Relational Psychotherapy

A Practical Guide To Control Your Emotions, Declutter Your Mind, Stop Overthinking And Master Your Relationship & Social Skills.

Ariana Huckaby

unless express consent of the Publisher is provided beforehand. Any additional rights reserved.

Furthermore, the information that can be found within the pages described forthwith shall be considered both accurate and truthful when it comes to the recounting of facts. As such, any use, correct or incorrect, of the provided information will render the Publisher free of responsibility as to the actions taken outside of their direct purview. Regardless, there are zero scenarios where the original author or the Publisher can be deemed liable in any fashion for any damages or hardships that may result from any of the information discussed herein.

Additionally, the information in the following pages is intended only for informational purposes and should thus be thought of as universal. As befitting its nature, it is presented without assurance regarding its prolonged validity or interim quality. Trademarks that are mentioned are done without written consent and can in no way be considered an endorsement from the trademark holder.

INTRODUCTION

The emerging Relational Tradition of Psychoanalytic and Psychodynamic Thinking become more difficult to catch briefly. Relational Psychotherapy believes that our ideas about ourselves, people, and the world are formed in relationships, and that we know how to cope with our feelings in relationships. While it is useful to explore these two concepts independently, both methods are strongly intertwined.

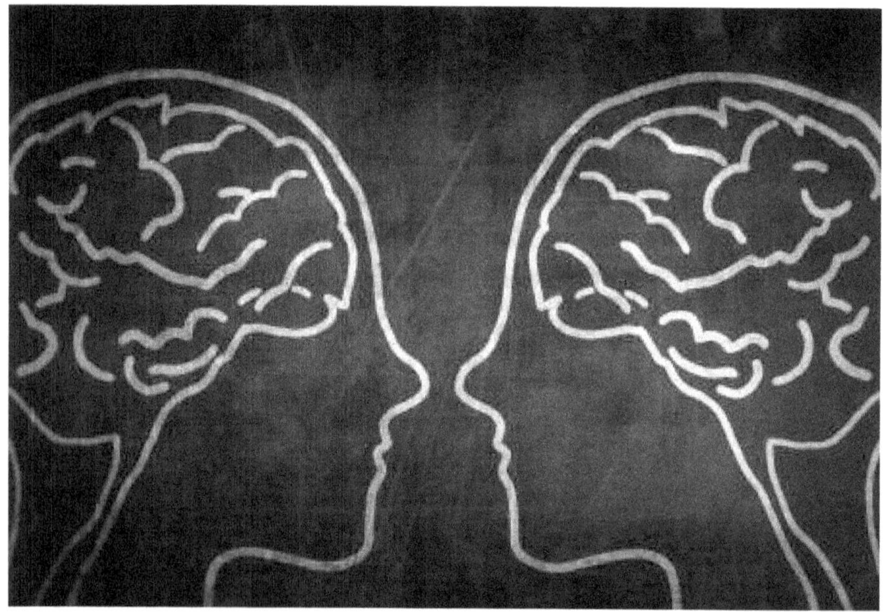

Our views about ourselves and the aspirations of others and the world are influenced by relationships. Most of these convictions, or prejudices, are formed in our early relationships. Some of these values have been freely offered to us (e.g. "Never trust a salesman, son!") and many others have been learned by observing the responses of others to themselves or circumstances (e.g. "Mommy must be upset because I am too insecure when I want her attention"). These grow into prejudices that affect how we see ourselves, others, and circumstances in which we find ourselves. Some of these beliefs were profoundly rooted and rarely consciously thought of, because they work out of our consciousness.

Some of these interactions have caused us to concentrate on what we see about ourselves as bad, or to reflect on excessively positive or negative characteristics of others (e.g. "She's too clever, she must think I'm stupid") or on overly positive or negative facets of the world in general (e.g. "going out is often stressful"). If we only concentrate on and highlight certain facets of a situation or experience, we end up with a narrow and restricted viewpoint and lack the ability to see things from their multiple possibilities. As you can guess, these accents and prejudices can lead to traumatic emotional and mental interactions that we can't exactly identify. To seek to sum it up in a sentence: we are denied the realities that are on the verge of knowledge of ourselves, others, and the universe, and the more reality we are denied, the more we struggle for it.

We've been living in an emotional world since birth. Our key caregivers are showing us how to control our feelings, whether they know it or not. Ideally, they respond consistently to our feelings, calming us when we're irritated, or responding with enthusiasm to our achievements.

However, where listening to children's feelings becomes too neglectful, too overbearing, too complicated, or too contradictory, one loses the sense of health, loyalty, and the opportunity to feel all right about what he or she feels. Such "unsafe" or "disorganized attachments" often hinder the child's own self-development. The infant is instilled with the guilt of not possessing his desires, which is when his ego is attended to.

This results in a personality that evolves by adjusting to the standards of others. In the case of too overlooked situations, one continues to ignore and mistrust some, as well as to reduce the need for some. In the case of too stifling situations, one becomes suspicious of others while at the same time feeling dependent on them.

These are strongly similar, if not one-in - the-same, interactions. If it's how we view the environment or how we learn to cope with our feelings, these exist mainly on non-verbal levels and inside relationships. What we expect from our perceptions of the universe, or how others react to our feelings, is mainly expressed, and thus occurs largely out of our consciousness (i.e. we experience what we understand, but we can't really relate about what we know).

These theories represent an immersive psychology about what happens outside of you and what happens inside of you. Some types in psychotherapy and psychiatry overemphasize what's going on internally (i.e. neurotransmitters, emotional thinking), leading individuals to ignore how relationships, even also one's society, may lead to their misery. It adds to so many people thinking that the problem is with them alone.

Relational experience tries to align the inside with the outside. As so much of this "real thinking" has led to our pain, Relational Therapy often views relationships as an outlet for recovery. The therapy partnership is a way to encourage such assumptions to emerge, to recognize them, and gradually to alleviate them so that they avoid reducing the possibilities that you might explore about the world and yourself. It is the mindset of inquiry in Relationship Therapy that removes objective judgement or the futile removal of the "other side of events" and opens you up to more reality.

CHAPTER ONE
WHAT IS RELATIONAL PSYCHOTHERAPY

Social psychotherapy is a powerful and effective therapeutic mechanism for people struggling and undergoing persistent mental, psychiatric and relational trauma.

The core theory of relational therapy is that attachment, interaction, and interdependence are innate in human experience and help clients recognize their own patterns of thinking, feeling, and perception, while also understanding the role and effect of important "others" in influencing their self-experience.

Relational therapy activates the right brain, influences the regulation of the left brain, conscious thought and contemplation.

Relational psychotherapy, a technique that can help individuals realize the role that relationships play in influencing daily experiences, seeks to help people understand trends that occur in their thoughts and feelings about themselves.

Based on the idea that healthy and satisfying relationships with other persons may help people sustain emotional well-being, this paradigm may be beneficial to people seeking therapy for a variety of reasons, but in particular to resolve long-term emotional distress, particularly when there is depression as a result of relationship issues.

Relational Psychotherapy is a branch of contemporary psychoanalytic psychotherapy that I find is most beneficial to the clients I see. It is a powerful and effective approach for dealing with people suffering from chronic mental, psychiatric and/or social trauma. This is based on the following concepts Emotional well-being relies on maintaining a good relationship with others.

Emotional distress is often embedded in cycles of social experience, past and present, which have the ability to demean and destroy the self. The relational therapist seeks to understand the particular self-experience of the individual in its social / relational context and to respond with empathy and sincere presence. Together, the client and therapist create a new, in-depth partnership that embraces, reinforces and encourages the client. Within this secure relationship, the person can comfortably re-experience and then find freedom from the powerful effects of past and present harmful relationships. Empowerment and development through interpersonal communication are both the mechanism and the aim of relational psychotherapy.

Relational therapists help clients to consider, on the one hand, their own habits of thinking and feeling about themselves and, on the other hand, the influence of important relationships, past and present, to form this self-experience. Through the indirect phase of social engagement, behavioral therapy reinforces and changes a client's sense of self, which in effect increases his or her faith and well-being in the community. In this approach to mediation and marriages, the relationship therapist takes seriously the inter-personal effect of power differentials and social problems such as race, age, religion, ethnicity, and sexual disparity. The concepts of relational psychotherapy are drawn from self-psychology, inter-subjectivity theory, behavioral psychoanalysis, psychodynamic cognitive theory, trauma theory, and feminist philosophies of psychotherapy, dealing with such problems as they occur in the client's life and clinical relationship.

HISTORY AND DEVELOPMENT

An integrative method of counseling, cognitive psychotherapy, was developed out of a synthesis of many psychological ideas and procedures. Which comprise self-psychology, cognitive psychoanalysis, and feminist psychotherapy theories. The work of Jean Baker Miller has led to the development of this method a variety of valuable ideas. Many notable people who have partnered together to establish this method include Janet Surrey, Judy Jordan and Irene Stiver, who have collaborated with the Jean Baker Miller Teaching Center at Wellesley College.

In the 1980s, there was a shift in the philosophy of counseling, moving away from merely analyzing inward interactions (intrasubjective) and towards a deeper view of the effect of relationships on human (intersubjective) interactions. Since then, relational psychotherapy has grown to become a commonly accepted clinical framework for many other types of counseling that focus on a person's interactions and the effect they can have on emotional and mental well-being.

CORE PRINCIPLES OF RELATIONAL PSYCHOTHERAPY

Relational psychotherapy is based on the concept that relationships with others are an essential part of mental well-being. Individuals who find it difficult to sustain stable and safe relationships may suffer a sense of disconnection in addition to a feeling of decreased self-esteem and general depression, which may have a negative effect on their sense of emotional well-being.

The philosophy of relational psychotherapy follows the following principles:• It is necessary for a person to have a rewarding and meaningful relationship with others around him in order to maintain mental wellbeing.

• Tension and emotional instability are often the result of past relationship interactions, and these issues that impede the full expression of the present self.

• The practitioner who administers behavioral psychotherapy offers an environment of empathic and attentiveness in order to ensure full disclosure of the interactions and incidents surrounding the person seeking care, as well as the impact they have had on both the relationship and the community.

• The therapist and the client in treatment work together to build a healthy, constructive and supportive friendship that can serve as a model for the future relationship that the individual wants to develop. Many interactions can be evaluated against this positive one to assess whether they are constructive or damaging.

HOW DOES RELATIONAL PSYCHOTHERAPY WORK

Relationship psychotherapy sessions usually stress the creation of social understanding. To order to do this, the psychiatrist and the client to treatment typically need to develop an awareness of the individual's disconnection techniques. Or the human contact forms that are used to drive people further. When established, the psychiatrist and the client will discuss the possible explanations for the use of these techniques. Transformation occurs as the therapist and the client create new psychological representations using the partner-person in a supportive partnership as a paradigm for a safe and stable partnership.

The primary goal of behavioral psychotherapy is to help people seeking help better understand how they communicate with others and how their individual behaviors can have an effect on their mental and emotional well-being. Therapists can also help individuals better understand and take into account the implications of inequalities in authority or inclusion, as well as the importance of social issues such as age, ethnicity, gender and history.

TRAINING AND CERTIFICATION

Similar psychotherapy educational is provided through a variety of specialist training programs and mental health centers. Of example, the American Psychological Association provides continued education that centers on behavioral psychotherapy. Many groups providing method training include the Toronto Center for Relational Psychotherapy, which delivers a structured curriculum for the use of relational psychotherapy, and the Jean Baker Miller Educational Institute, which conducts research and facilitates seminars and professional training. When certain events, interactions, and/or values impair a person's ability to derive pleasure and gratification from life, counseling can often help a person to gain insight and resolve a situation or relationship.

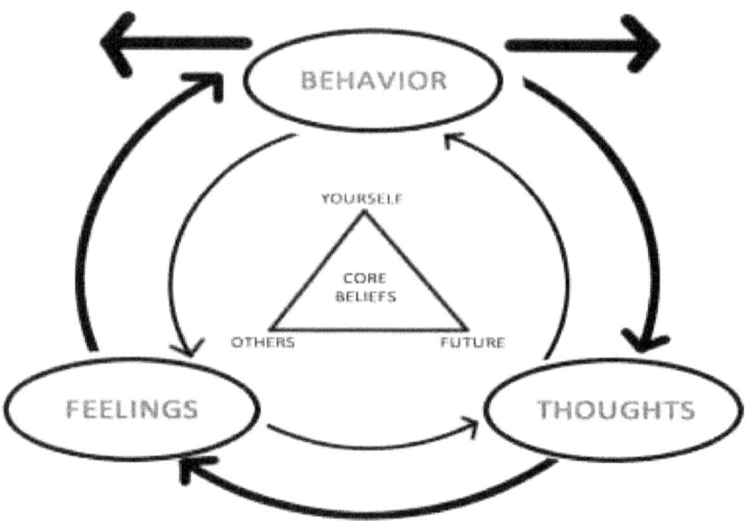

Relational theory, which proposes that the sense of connectedness generated by healthy relationships is a crucial aspect of human well-being, indicates that when there is no such bond, mental and emotional problems can emerge. The primary goal of this intervention is to address these concerns and enable people seeking treatment to become more able to develop healthy, long-lasting relationships. Mutual understanding and sincerity, as demonstrated through a therapeutic relationship, will help to achieve this goal.

When other events, interactions, and/or values impair a individual's desire to derive pleasure and gratification from life, counseling may also allow a person to obtain perspective and resolve a situation or relationship.

This approach is generally useful to individuals in resolving the consequences of marital problems, such as family issues and intimate relationship complications, new life circumstances, or school and job issues. Relational psychotherapy may also be useful to those who find emotional control overwhelming, and has also been shown to be effective in the management of interpersonal problems caused by anxiety, fatigue, or depression.

ISSUES AND LIMITATIONS

While behavioral psychotherapy may be effective in the treatment of a wide range of concerns, this technique may not be prescribed for people with avoidable personality traits.

Furthermore, the implementation of formal curriculum for students may be difficult, as this methodology is largely based on philosophy rather than on the use of specific techniques.

While a good professional interaction between the psychiatrist and the client in care is an essential component of all forms of therapy, relationship therapy stresses the partnership between the therapist and the individual as being cooperative and constructive. Therefore, therapists who have been trained to take a more neutral approach or to take on a specialist position may have some difficulties in using behavioral psychotherapy, as it puts particular importance on the therapist's reaction and cooperation.

MAIN PRINCIPLES IN RELATIONSHIP THERAPY

Here are some of the topics that your behavioral therapist will be focusing on and how it can benefit you.

1. It's linking matters.

Emotional and psychological well-being implies that we have a healthy, trustworthy and rewarding relationship with others. We've got to feel linked.

Relational counseling makes you think, how do I respond to others? How am I supposed to try to communicate, is it working, and if not, why not?

2. Disconnection leads to mental health problems.

If we continually undermine the relation, it results in pain and problems like depression, anxiety, and disease.

3. The secret is credibility.

We need to understand how to be ourselves in relationships so that they can be through.

Who are you, and how would your relationships change if you paid that forward?

4. The history is what tells our present.

Past partnerships influence the decisions we make regarding our present and future partnerships. And what we've experienced in the past has an effect on how we behave with people in the current.

How did you learn the view from which you see all relationships? Is that true? What would the friendship be if you started making assumptions about it?

5. Social and cultural influences have an effect on your way of being around others.

Unlike other forms of therapy, relational therapy focuses on how issues like history, race, class and gender influence the patterns of control between you and others.

Does your social and cultural history mean that you don't owe others a chance? Or are they saying they're not going to give you one? How's that going to cause you issues and upset?

6. The interaction between the client and the therapist is very critical.

The' therapeutic bond' that you have with your psychiatrist will serve as a model for you on how to repair other relationships in your life, as well as a safe space to try out new ways of communicating.

How are you going to know when to trust? And what would happen to your friendship if you were open and relaxed with others as you continue to be with your therapist?

THE ADVANTAGES OF RELATIONAL THERAPY

Maybe one of the easiest ways to understand' What is relational therapy?It would be to look at what it seeks to bring to customers.

• More mental and emotional strength

• More inspiration inside relationships and life itself

• Fewer power struggles with others

• More fulfilling relationships

• Stop driving people away

• Improve the ability to trust

• Increased self-esteem

• Improved self-understanding.

HOW IS RELATIONAL THERAPY DIFFERENT THAN OTHER THERAPY

Relational therapy is the same as other types of talk therapy as it is dealing with how your past experiences negatively affect your way of being in the now, and how you can become more responsive to others.

But it's different from some more conventional talk therapy because:

• It focuses only on how you respond

• This relates pain, anxiety and depression to an inability to connect well with others

• It brings social and cultural factors into account

• It sets a very strong emphasis on the relationship between the individual and therapist.

CHAPTER THREE
WHAT SORTS OF ISSUES CAN RELATIONAL THERAPY HELP WITH

The following are all things behavioral counseling may be useful for:

ANXIETY

Tension is a sense of pressure that has a specific source or purpose. Life throws something away from you, or you make a difficult decision, and the resulting sense of frustration, anxiety, and concern is stress.

Stress can, of course, be unreasonable–you can become so overwhelmed and disturbed by your feelings that you have distorted, emotional thoughts. But it's logical in the way that you know why you're going through it. So it's under your influence in this way.

Anxiety, on the other hand, is a sense of anxiety and stress that seems to have no exact cause. Even if you're trying to put it down to one thing, you're struggling with that thing, and the feeling doesn't go away. And there's anxiety under the emotional present, not shocking because you feel so helpless to rationalize what you're feeling.

ANXIETY SYMPTOMS

Sense of anxiety. Even if it doesn't make sense to feel scared, anxiety will leave you feeling some kind of fear, even lower forms of terror or unease.

Feeling out of reach, man. You feel like you don't have any power over your life and feelings and you can't figure out just why you feel so scared and nervous.

A sense of helplessness. Without realizing what might stop the feelings you're having, you might begin to feel completely overwhelmed.

Tension, guy. This may include physical symptoms such as headache and muscle pain.

Obsessing what you're talking for. Fear is so extreme that you can often continue to have' anxiety over anxiety,' exacerbating what you're still dealing with.

Stress.Stress. Overwhelm can intensify into fear, or even panic attacks. Panic attacks have physical symptoms such as a trembling, a rapid sensation of heat or cold, a squeezing of the throat, and a pulse.

BODY DYSMORPHIA

Body dysmorphic disorder (BDD), sometimes known to as' body dysmorphia,' is an anxiety disorder about how you appear.

It makes you persistently depressed and disturbed because you view your face, or part of your body, in a negative way and as separate from what it really is. Either the real physical defect is extremely exaggerated, or it is absolutely imaginable.

BDD is sometimes compared to obsessive compulsive disorder, because it can cause you to build rituals of trying to' hide' your perceived imperfection or cope with the discomfort that it gives you. What does body dysmorphic disorder look like?

Body dysmorphia can include some part of your body, and may indicate that you have a false impression of your height, proportion, or disfigurement of some kind. Examples of BDDs are:

• imagining that you are overweight and' big' when you have a normal body image

• assuming that you are too short or not strong enough and need to work out a lot harder (sometimes named' muscle dysmorphia')

• worried nonstop that everyone is constantly looking at your uneven eyebrows / crooked nose / thin hair / fat' arms etc

• fearing that you are the ugliest person anywhere you go

• fear.

SYMPTOMS OF BODY DYSMORPHIC DISORDER

• spending a few hours each day worrying poorly about your supposed physical defect

• Constantly comparing yourself to others

• feeling anxious when faced with social circumstances

• creating different habits to avoid social interaction or help you feel better about your' defect'

• Not wanting people to look at you

• Intense feelings of embarrassment and embarrassment.

Periods of always looking in the mirror or looking at your' defect,' or ignoring all mirrors at all Wasting a lot of time in figuring out ways to cover up and downplay the' defect,' such as dressing a certain way or using other kinds of makeup, spend a lot of time' fixing' the defects, such as over-exercise, dieting, taking supplements, trying' treatments' and doing research.

It's not ego, but body dysmorphia isn't.

People with body dysmorphia don't feel good about themselves unconsciously, or want to be better. They are seriously flawed in their warped way of thinking and would prefer to be just' human.'

It's not just a matter of getting publicity.

BDD sufferers live with constant negative thoughts and fears in their minds,And often people with body dysmorphia experience such guilt and fear that they conceal their thoughts about themselves from others rather than talk about them.

It's not just a low self-esteem.

Body dysmorphia certainly involves low self-esteem, but it's not going to be fixed by' pep talk.' Genetic and behavioral abnormalities that may be related to past traumas are also considered to be likely.

It's not just' having a bad day.'

If you have body dysmorphia, anxiety about the way you look is relentless and constant.

It's not a nerve anorexia.

Anorexia nervosa may cause body dysmorphia. But there are two different disorders, with anorexia in the heart about weight and power, and BDD for self-perception and anxiety.

DEPRESSION

In addition, understanding the difference between depression and grief is very important.

It means you don't ignore a serious mental condition because you think it's just a bad mood. It also says, if you're really depressed, you're not going to panic.

What's the SADNESS?

Sadness is an emotion that is actually a normal, natural, healthy response to certain parts of life. Now and again, we can't stop feeling depressed. And if we didn't feel depressed sometimes, how would we know what happiness is in comparison?

Sadness allows us to decide what matters to us, what we want and what we don't like. And it allows one to handle traumatic events like defeat and disappointment.

When we allow ourselves to feel sorrow in its entirety, instead of denying it or fighting it off? And let it pass through us, instead of being trapped in it and feeling like a victim? Sadness can even feel more invigorating, like a strong rainstorm passing in.

We seem to ask exactly when we feel depressed. It's going to be a certain, measurable experience or a collection of experiences behind the emotions.

And although depression may last for a few days or weeks, depending on its cause, it will eventually leave.

Sadness will come and go as well, as if we were in mourning, and we had sad days interspersed with feeling all right.

Depression is a feeling of being far from a good part of life.

It is called a' maladaptive' action because it is an inefficient way of coping with it. It keeps us from adjusting to life, or it makes our days worse.

Depression may cause depression, but is often less positive than feeling sad or feeling anything at all. Most sufferers talk about feeling cold. Depression often tends to come with physical symptoms, such as tiredness, brain fog, and a decrease of appetite.

Even, when we feel depressed, we can have no idea why. It might be as if we had a migraine, or we abruptly dropped down a pit. Or it may feel illogical, with a little stuff going on, and we feel like it's the end of the planet.

Depression appears to be very persistent. We're always so sad all the time, no matter how badly we want a break, and it's going on for six weeks, several months, or even years.

STRESS

Some stress, caused by regular life challenges, is unavoidable. And while feeling nervous about a work presentation or frustrated by a parent teacher meeting gone wrong is not fun, nobody would compare it to the challenge that is depression.

Severe stress, however, is a different story. As anyone who has suffered chronic stress knows, with the resulting mood swings, sleeplessness, and low of self-esteem it can bring, the line between stress and depression can start to feel a little blurred.

Stress is the feeling that you are under too much mental or emotional pressure. It is triggered by something in your life happening that feels too much for you personally to handle, regardless of whether others can or can't. This might be a work issue, dealing with relationship conflict, or debt problems.

Stress isn't an illness or a disorder, but it can develop into one if it is left to become chronic.

While a little bit of stress is normal and can have positive results like getting you motivated or taking useful risks in the workplace too much stress over too long of a period can begin to negatively affect all parts of your life.

You might find it harder to function and concentrate at work, lose interest in your social life, and find yourself being irritable with those you love. Physically perhaps you aren't sleeping well, are under or overeating, and have signs of muscle tension including headaches and stomachaches. At worse, it can lead to high blood pressure and other serious health issues.

Stress also affects neurotransmitters and hormones including cortisol that, while it can leave you sometimes 'buzzed' in a way that feels good, are taxing on the body and can lead to cycles of feeling high then crashing.

What do Stress and Depression Have in Common?

Any tension, triggered by daily life struggles, is unavoidable. So while it's not fun to feel worried about a work interview or upset about a parent teacher meeting gone bad, nobody can equate that to the difficulty of depression.

Extreme pain, though, is another matter. As someone who has experienced constant depression should know, with the associated mood swings, sleeplessness, and poor self-esteem

• Both are individuals (it is not another that causes stress or depression in one person)

• They affect your energy levels

• Influence mood

• Sleep patterns are disturbed

• Eating patterns may be disrupted (overeating or overeating)

• You are not yourself

• May have difficulty working properly

• Can be frustrating

• You may not be interested in hanging out with friends and family

• They can both feel overwhelming

• You may not be able to concentrate

• Both affect the body's stress response mechanism

• Both are known to affect the brain in a similar way

LONELINESS

With the number of people experiencing feeling alone having doubled over the past 30 years, it's now considered a "singleness pandemic." In America, 40% of people now class themselves as struggling with depression. In the United Kingdom, the Major Lottery Fund and local councils are also providing support to aid those feeling vulnerable and alone, particularly the elderly.

There's nothing wrong with being alone, of course. The introverts among us are predisposed to enjoy their own company over being in a crowd, and that is completely safe.

Feeling lonely is special, not about whether you're with other friends or by yourself at all. It's about how you want to be related to others and how much you really are. That's why you can feel lonely with your partner or in a crowd.

It's a fallacy to believe that having a lot of friends means you're not alone. Loneliness is less about quantity and more about lack of quality contact, the kind that makes us feel connected, appreciated and willing to share.

And isolation is a very serious psychological problem. Overcoming isolation is crucial because being left unchecked can lead to anxiety, addictions like alcoholism, and poor sleep habits. A study at the University of Chicago looking at how isolation impacts the immune system has found an increased risk of cancer and stroke.

Not that isolation is evil. Often discovering our own need for others can contribute to a deeper understanding of what life means to us. In the very least, it allows us to be humble and appreciate the friendship we have. And coping with depression can be safe now and then.

LOW SELF-ESTEEM

Suicidal Thoughts–The Hidden Source of The Poor Self-Esteem. It's real that we all have depressive feelings when life is hard and we feel frustrated.

But maybe the feelings that cause the most harm are not the great despairing ones, but the steady stream of pessimistic feelings that you might have on a regular basis without even knowing it.

But they're just the feelings, what's the big deal?

Constant pessimistic thoughts may be so entrenched that we don't really know when we're doing something until we take the effort to consider to a technique like mindfulness. Since we're used to pessimistic thoughts, it's easy to believe that it's benevolent.

Yet pessimistic thinking leads to negative thoughts, it leads to bad decisions in life (known as negative thought). So the more cynical your feelings, the more likely it is that you will not take action that will lead to a future that you really like.

And negative thinking leads to low moods and often to depression.

One of the key reasons for this is that poor thought provides a ideal atmosphere for low self-esteem to prosper.

Negative thinking habits that destroy your self-esteem As soon as you start listening to your feelings, these are the most common-lowering negative thoughts you'll usually find first: putting yourself down (you look overweight, you're too slow)

• Pessimistic core beliefs (I'm not good, I'm not as smart as other people, I'm never going to win)

• Comparing yourself to others (I'm never going to be as good as hi).

EATING DISORDERS

Psychology also focuses on feelings and habits related to eating disorders. For example, cognitive behavioral therapy (CBT) can concentrate on how critical thoughts about the body or food triggers eating disorders.

Yet research also suggests that part of what causes you to have a eating disorder is subconscious feelings that may have less to do about the body or diet but rather in the overall way you view the world and yourself.

Those are what you consider to be your true convictions.

What are the core beliefs?

Core beliefs are established in childhood. These are conclusions that we make about ourselves, others, and the universe when we find a error as a matter of fact.

Such values are rooted in our unconscious, where they control the decisions we make in life, before we make the effort to dig them out and change them.

Of course, some of us are fortunate enough to have an upbringing that leads to strong core beliefs that make it easier for adults to handle.

But many of us end up with negative or misadaptative (or optimistic) core beliefs. These can come from a childhood where we feel unloved, faced ridicule, could not trust the people around us, or experienced trauma or violence.

An example of a common negative core belief is' I'm unlovable.' This could happen if, say, a parent went away without warning for a long time, and your childlike brain thought it was your fault. And, as an adult, when someone wants to love you, you're going to find ways to undermine the relationship to' prove' that your intuition is correct. Perhaps one of these ways is to overeat so much that the body is repulsing others.

Core beliefs and eating disorders A number of studies have been done on this subject, all suggesting that people with eating disorders have more negative core beliefs than those who do not.

A well-known 2006 review was applied beyond previous research and was the first to include people with EDNOS syndrome (eating disorder not otherwise specified). The study looked at 106 people with eating disorders and 27 non-food disorders. It has established that the type and severity of one's eating disorder is directly related to core beliefs.

Binge eating disorder participants were found to have many misadaptive behaviors, but most were reported in patients with anorexia and bulimia. In addition, in those who purged or fasted, it was discovered that core beliefs were even a predictor of how often someone might use diarrhea, laxatives, or fasting.

So then, what kind of core beliefs would be linked to eating disorder?

Studies on core beliefs and eating disorders included the following views (with possible examples in brackets): • Defectiveness / shame (I'm not perfect, I'm weak, I'm unlovable, I'm ugly...) • Insufficient self-control (I'm worthless, I can't manage, I can't control anything...) • Failure to achieve (I'm not fine, I'm dumb, everybody else is greater than me...) • Entitlement (I can't control anything...)

• Dependence / incompetence (I'm weak, I can't handle life, being alone is terrifying, growing up is scary)• Vulnerability (bad things still happen, I draw danger) • Emotional repression (I don't deserve to have feelings, you have to hide your true self in order to be cherished, depression or anger make you a bad person, if I reveal my emotions, bad things will happen to me or others) • Emotional deficiency (I don't deserve to be...

• Abandonment / Instability (everyone I love leaves me, it's bad to love someone as they leave, if people leave me, I'll die).

• Mistrust / misuse (everyone just uses me, you can't trust anyone to really be there for you)• Subjugation (I have to do what people say or negative things are going to happen) • Self-sacrifice (I have to set myself aside to help everyone, others care more than me) • Unrelenting expectations (I have to try to be the best, you have to be the best or you're nothing) How can these core beliefs trigger eating?

Again, we tend to behave in ways that' prove' our core beliefs are' true.' So it might be that your eating disorder is a way to prove your theory true. "I am deficient and a mess, and the eating disorder confirms that." But in many situations, eating disorders are used to manipulate and conceal our core beliefs. Another study at the University of London showed that the number of times someone binds to food was related to a confidence in emotional inhibition. Vomiting, on the other hand, was connected to the belief in defectiveness and guilt.

TRUST ISSUES

Honesty is a term that we can throw around so quickly. "I don't like anyone." "Why am I supposed to trust you?". "You must trust yourself before you can trust others."

But what does IS faith, really? And why is it so important when it comes to emotional well-being?

What's the trust?

It's a huge concept, with meanings that change depending on the context within which it is defined. And in the field of psychology?

Morton Deutsch, one of the pioneers of conflict resolution, was one of the first psychologists to try to establish trust. At one point, he called it "faith that a person can see what is expected from another rather than what is anticipated." More recently, psychologists at Cornell University in America debated whether trust was really about optimistic hopes or whether it was really just a social norm. Trusting others is what we think we're going to do.

Perhaps faith is a combination of both–a conviction and a practiced conduct. What is certain is that confidence is a natural instinct to live, as well as a driving force that keeps us going forward in life.

OTHER COMPONENTS OF TRUST Vulnerability Feelings Trust involves risk. You place the desired outcome in the hands of another human, and this ensures that you are leaving yourself vulnerable, and you may feel fear and worry.

Co-operation and Compromise Trust means trusting and wanting others to do something for your well-being, often missing out on what they desired for themselves in order to maintain trust within the relationship. Of example, they believe that you want them to be comfortable, too, and sometimes compromise on the well-being of the relationship itself.

Self-confidence It's not just about trusting the other guy, it's about trusting yourself. If you don't believe like you need to be helped, it's hard to trust anyone.

Interdependence Trust can be seen as an interdependence bond. This ensures that both of you can take care of yourself if necessary, but choose to support each other and work together for a better result.

WORKPLACE ISSUES

Psychologists and social scientists have been raising the red flag for stress at work for decades now. The last major government survey in 2012 found that 40% of workers in the United Kingdom faced work-related stress.

But, while the workforce certainly has its problems, is it really the only cause of rising rates of stress-related illness in the United Kingdom, or are we missing a trick? If there's anything to do with a new study causing a stir, the answer is a resounding yes, we are.

The research, undertaken by Penn State University in America, showed that being at work in many ways is good for our health, and our tension can come from our home life instead.

Researchers found that cortisol, a hormone produced by the body in response to stress, was much lower in participants when they were at work than when they were at home. One imagines that this news is hardly shocking for many, especially working mothers among us (the study found that while both men and women find the workplace more calming, women more so). That said, lower work stress rates were observed in people who both did and did not have children, while those who had children had a greater difference in their cortisol levels between work and home.

Of example, there are a number of factors to keep in mind before you get depressed at home tonight about your stress levels! The study included only a very small group of 122 people, similar to the British government survey with a sample group of over one million. We don't know how many of those participants actually took home research and, to top it off, the participants measured cortisol levels themselves, leaving room for error. And almost all the participants feel less anxious on the weekends than during the week, suggesting that it is the jonglage of work and stress that is at the heart of the matter.

And if you make a high wage, the findings didn't hold–the study showed that those who made a high salary had the same level of stress at work and at home. This is still a very interesting finding. It demonstrates the depression did not get worse in the workplace, and confirms that life is not the intense danger zone that we like to talk of.

Despite the small size and variables of the study, it actually measured the body's reactions to stress, rather than just carrying out work-related stress questionnaires, which make it groundbreaking. We are sure to see more research questioning the stress of the workplace in the future.

Psychotherapy is a form of treatment for a number of psychiatric illnesses that has been used in psychology for decades.

According to the American Psychological Association (APA), psychotherapy can be described as "collaborative care between an patient and a psychologist" where the psychologist uses "scientifically proven techniques to help people develop safer, more productive behaviors."

For our purposes, psychotherapy can be described as therapeutic care for a number of mental health conditions that may or may not be done in combination with medicinal therapy.

PSYCHOTHERAPY TECHNIQUES, TOOLS & EXERCISES

A new article is a generalized approach that psychotherapists can use to perform effective meetings. This approach is broken down into four steps:• Relating: this involves empathy for the patient's self-esteem and challenges, as well as being compassionate.

• Exploring: This involves paying attention to what the client says (as well as what they don't say) and their body language, as well as posing questions to fully appreciate the client and explain the inconsistencies.

• Explaining: This involves understanding the cognitive biases of the client and the therapist can influence the conversation, as well as acknowledging any other variables (sociological, behavioral, psychological, etc.) that could form the client's behavior, and then eventually telling the client whether or not they agree with your opinions and assumptions.

• Intervening: It involves communicating one's views to the client so that they can agree or disagree with them, not encouraging the client's disruptive or deceptive actions, and advising the client how to deal with their issues (such as coping skills).

One problem with psychotherapy is that therapists usually underestimate the number of people that quit care without help or at risk of decline. The first step in addressing this problem is to make clinicians aware of the difference between how they believe therapy is going and how the person is currently progressing.

Another approach to do this is through the OutcomeQuestionnaire-45(OQ-45), a 45-question self-assessment that clients should complete at the end of each session to monitor their clinical success. If therapists give clients this alternative, they can more quickly identify clients in need of changed treatment plans.

There is also a Youth ResultQuestionnaire-30 (Y-OQ-30) for children and adolescents, which can be done either by the individual or their parent(s). By using these methods, psychotherapists can ensure that their treatment plans are successful and, if they are not, can change them.

HOW TO DEAL WITH RESISTANCE IN PSYCHOTHERAPY

One way to deal with resistance in psychotherapy is for the psychiatrist to encourage the client for input at the end of each session and to try to change their treatment plan in response to that feedback. For example, certain clients whose input was received suggested that their psychiatrist did not understand their circumstances because of their own power as a therapist. The psychiatrist was then able to recognize this and integrate it into their care so that they could approach their client from a more honest and open viewpoint.

Another study of resistance in psychotherapy focused specifically on in-session anxiety. Some participants made clients complete post-session questionnaires asking them to recognize any in-session pain they encountered. From there, the clinicians were more careful to track in-session anxiety and addressed this discomfort with their counselor as they realized it was becoming a matter of concern. When in-session depression was reported and addressed, clients attended further recovery sessions and achieved better post-therapy outcomes.

This notion is reflected in the explanation of the case study of a man who sought treatment for anger issues at the urging of his father. When the psychiatrist experienced intense opposition from the client, she immediately interrupted the therapy and (politely) approached him about his frustration, helping the client to know he was being attended to. From there, the psychiatrist allowed the client greater flexibility by encouraging him to organize the treatment himself, at which point he became less defensive and was finally able to solve some of his problems (with several psychotherapy sessions).

The principle of adaptability is a common thread in all three of these articles. In all cases, clinicians met with resistance as they ran the sessions of the book and were somewhat restrictive. By getting direct feedback from the client, the therapists have been able to modify their therapy plans to address the client's needs, and from there they have faced less opposition.

Since psychotherapy is intended to be an individualized procedure, the ability to adapt a treatment plan is vital for any practitioner who experiences opposition.

THE BEST PSYCHOTHERAPY

Approaches though multiple psychotherapy interventions may be effective for different people and for different disorders, there are the best-proven psychotherapy interventions out there.

Three psychotherapy treatment plans listed as empirically supported therapies (ESTs) are cognitive behavioral therapy (CBT), psychodynamic psychotherapy, and therapeutic psychotherapy (Feinstein et al., 2015). CBT "helps you recognise unhealthful, negative beliefs and habits and substitute them with good, positive ones." Psychodynamic psychotherapy consists of "enhancing your understanding of unconscious thoughts and behaviors, developing new insights into your motives and resolving conflicts," while positive psychotherapy "enhances your ability to cope with stress and difficult situations."

Psychotherapy integrating facets of mindfulness-based stress reduction (MBSR) has been shown to be effective in reducing signs of stress and anxiety. MBSR aims to help you "build a capacity to deal more effectively with both short-term and long-term stressful situations." This is an interesting finding, because the mindfulness and instruction of MBSR can quickly be integrated into conventional psychotherapy.

Short-term psychodynamic therapy with metallization-based therapy (STMBP) has been shown to be effective treatment for major depressive disorder (MDD), metallization-based therapy (MBT) seeks to "[help] patients to distinguish and separate their own thoughts and feelings from those around them." This is another example of how quick application to conventional psychotherapy practice will make it useful for more individuals.

Psilocybin-assisted psychotherapy has been shown to be effective in reducing signs of stress and anxiety in cancer patients. There, psilocybin-assisted psychotherapy applied to a lengthy psychotherapy session during which psilocybin was given to the client. Unlike most psychotherapy, psilocybin-assisted psychotherapy is expected to consist of only one session, although that session may be part of a longer, multi-sessional treatment plan.

Interpersonal psychotherapy (IPT) has been shown to reduce depressive symptoms in teenagers. IPT "focuses on discussing your current relationship with other people to improve your interpersonal skills." IPT can be effective in treating conditions that lead to social deficits, as well as marriage and family therapy.

Cognitive hypnotherapy (CH) has been shown to be effective in the management of anger problems. Cognitive hypnotherapy is a "CBT hypnosis incorporation" that began as a way to use hypnosis to treat depression. This is a good example of how conventional therapeutic theories (such as hypnosis) can be made more palatable to skeptics by convergence with more current, empirically supported therapies.

Dialectic behavioral therapy (DBT) has been shown to be effective in reducing suicidal ideation as well as stress and anxiety symptoms in combat veterans. Dialectical behavioral therapy is "a form of CBT that incorporates coping skills to help you manage stress, control feelings, and strengthen relationships with others." Although DBT is an extension of CBT, it is commonly used to deserve its own description.

A type of art therapy called short-clay art therapy (CAT) has been shown to be effective in improving the mental health of participants with MDD, art therapy is a' integrative mental health and human services profession that enriches the lives of individuals, families and communities through active art-, creative processes, applied psychological theory, and human experience in the field of psychotherapy. Art Therapy can help teenagers, teens, and less vocal-expressive people get more out of psychotherapy than conventional talk therapy.

CHAPTER FIVE

DIFFICULT PART OF RELATIONAL PSYCHOTHERAPY

Relationships aren't that easy. They can often be chaotic and hurtful, yet at the same time rewarding, insightful and significant. Human beings are complex creatures, so the relationships between two or more of them will become much more complicated. Because of this, there is no one way to make "right" relationships. This is true for all of our partnerships—with our parents, families, family, colleagues, husbands, wives, roommates, teachers, employers, supervisors, and strangers. "Relationship difficulties" are usually understood to be conflicts in a pair or another relational arrangement. "Relational challenges" refers to obstacles, conflicts or concerns that are inherent in the way we respond to others, taking "relationships" in a broad sense.

Because there are many forms of interactions that could stimulate and interact with different parts of us, there are a wide range of issues that could be called "relative obstacles." These could include things such as anxiety in social situations, inability to feel comfortable in intimate relationships, or difficulties that set boundaries with others. What we feel about our relationships has a major impact on how we feel about ourselves. In reality, in the first years of our lives, we relied on relationships to learn how to accept and value ourselves

WE ARE WIRED FOR RELATIONSHIPS

We come to this world in a very vulnerable state, totally dependent on others to thrive. Connecting and feeling connected to others is a biological imperative as it guarantees our existence. In fact, we try commitment and need others not only to ensure our physical security, but to ensure our mental and moral well-being.

One of the most important jobs our parents have in our childhood is helping us to make sense of our internal and external environment. No human being is born to know what rage, sorrow, suffering, happiness, or joy is. It is through the responses of our parents and other carers that we begin to understand our own thoughts and emotions and, in doing so, we begin to develop a sense of who we are.

It is in these early relationships that we first know about ourselves, about others, and what it means to be in a relationship. For starters, we may read about ourselves to feel like we are lovable, deserving, and deserving. Others, if they can be confident, embrace our emotions, or soothe us while we are in pain. With regard to relationships, we may come to trust that our desires can be articulated and met, that a close relationship can withstand conflict, or that can have our own thoughts and still be accepted.

WHAT CAN GO WRONG

Relationships are complex and problems are expected to emerge. There is no such thing as a perfect relationship; the problem is not so much how to avoid conflict and breakup, but how to progress towards reconciliation and recovery. That said, generally the problems we're grappling with as adults are ingrained in our previous relationships, those we've had with our family of origin. For better or worse, the period of time played a key role in influencing who we are, determining our personalities, and how we respond to others.

Have we grown up in an environment that values our borders? We were allowed to have our own thoughts and to share them even if they were awkward for the adults around us? Have we provided the support we needed to make sense of our own thoughts and emotions? Would we feel that the people we counted on saw, learned, recognized, and understood? Have we felt safe? How did we learn about sex, friendship, and marriages, from what we saw and witnessed at home?

The answers to these questions are complicated and are the result of a number of factors. One important aspect to take into account is the contrast that our parents have felt between being close enough to be attentive and helpful and encouraging us to become confident and self-sufficient. For many individuals, their childhood history was characterized by indifference or enmeshment. Their careers were physically or emotionally unavailable or had weak boundaries. Such encounters may be stressful given that they may have been perceived as daunting.

As a result, they formed an insecure commitment to others, in which they would feel very nervous about the continuity of relationships, or contempt for their value and their own feelings. We internalize others and our interactions with them, and those internalized statistics can tend to have an effect (consciously or not) on how we feel about ourselves and how we respond to others. The problem becomes more complicated when there is any sort of violence or environmental threat. Adverse childhood experiences have a negative impact on our growth and on our social, emotional and physical well-being.

THERE ARE MANY DIFFICULTIES

The challenges that people face as a result of these encounters can be very complex. We can find it difficult to set boundaries, communicate our desires, participate in conflict, trust, be sensitive, express or receive love. We may feel lonely even when we are not alone, we may find ourselves easily depressed or disenchanted, or we may rely on the affirmation of others to feel worthy. They also replicate behaviors, often unintentionally, such as trying to manage or influence others, engaging in toxic relationships, or becoming caregivers of others.

A lot of times the thing we want is the one we're scared of. We want to be loved, but we feel uncomfortable when someone shows love and care for us. We may long for friendship and attachment, but at the same time we are nervous or scared to let other people in.

Some of these behaviors and problems are of evolutionary nature and can be traced back to our early relationships and attachments. Our entire identity is partly formed and structured as a result of our interactions in early relationships. Such effects are the "natural" results of encounters that were hurtful or threatening, of wounds that remained open. In reality, these problems may have the potential to respond to, or defend ourselves from, our climate. For example, someone might become very controlling as a response to deep-seated insecurities produced by an unresponsive parent. Or someone else may easily feel resentful about not having a voice, because he's never been allowed to say so.

We tend to repeat the things that we have not really experienced or worked through, whether it means grieving a death, remembering a desire or a craving, or coping with feelings of anger or pain. The less we learn how our history stays with us, how we internalized our most important relationships, the more likely we are to replicate behaviors and turn those internalized memories onto others.

Traumatic relationships are not reserved for what happened in our youth. Our interactions as adults can have a great impact, too. Experience deception, frustration, or heartbreak can also have a profound impact on ourselves and our relationships. Of starters, maybe being betrayed by a romantic or business partner made it almost impossible to trust someone else again. However, the foundation for our ability to deal with these situations, including the way we see ourselves and others, has been laid down in our first few years of life. The experiences that followed were built on the top of the foundation. This is especially true if we have spent a long time without allowing ourselves to notice, experience, and handle injuries, longings, hurts, worries, sorrow, and other emotions that are too painful to see in the mind.

HOW WE RELATE TO OURSELVES IS IMPORTANT

Are we blunt and judgmental in our actions? Were we constantly putting ourselves down? Does it seem that even minor things make us doubt our ability or self-esteem? Do we believe we're bad, and if others actually knew us, they'd run away? Can we like our own thoughts and abilities? Do we agree that our needs are legitimate and that they need to be met?

A very important part of how we respond to others, whether they be family ones, relatives, peers or acquaintances, is how we respond to ourselves. The experiences and connections that we have had with our parents and other important people in our lives play a significant role in the creation of our sense of self, in how we understand who we are, and how we think and feel about ourselves. Such partnerships may also have an effect on what Should be achieved.

WHAT CAN WE DO

Often, individuals participate in marriage or family therapy to give the those concerned an chance to explore the complexities of their partnership. However, moving around behavioral problems does not always entail this set-up. It's hard to work on our relationship with others without going through the connection we have with ourselves.

This work usually includes raising awareness, empathy, acceptance and love of emotions, opinions, disagreements, interests, and aspects of ourselves that we have learnt to conceal or dislike. The goal is to increase our understanding and our capacity to understand who we are-to recognize and accept all aspects of ourselves-and where we come from. This will encourage us to find new ways to feel and think about ourselves and, in this way, to find new ways to be and to connect to others.

Relational injury and accidents through maturity can also have a significant impact on all of our relationships. Similarly, new relationships can also lead to recovery, reparation, and development. Partners and friends will give us a different relationship perspective if we are open to receiving it and willing to work on our unresolved or unprocessed problems.

Relationship with a psychiatrist can be a very critical tool for doing this research. When it comes to relationship problems, the strength of counseling derives from seeing it as an interaction between two human beings. It's a kind of friendship like no other. Therapy offers an opportunity to identify and analyze the behavioral dynamics that you participate in, when they inevitably-if you give enough time-emerge in a therapeutic relationship. It creates space to discuss the responses you may have to yourself and your therapist, and to move through times of closeness and disconnection. We can not change the past, but you can change the relationship that they have with it by having the opportunity to feel self-awareness, appreciation, approval, confidence and independence.

ADVANTAGES IN BEHAVIORAL PSYCHOTHERAPY

Most people think about psychotherapy purely as therapy. In addition, the term psychotherapy is used to describe a range of talk treatments to treat mental, physical, personal and psychological problems.

It requires a commitment to a variety of meetings with a licensed mental health provider, allowing a partnership to be formed between the psychiatrist and the patient.

This relationship focuses on helping a person to deal with or escape factors that contribute to his or her illness, with the overall goal of personal development and self-understanding. Like all other medical treatment, it has benefits and drawbacks.

Psychotherapy is widely used for treating patients with depression. It has been shown to be effective in the treatment of mild to moderate symptoms and can be combined with substance therapy to treat all levels of depression.

Participation in psychotherapy offers a number of advantages. For them, it's good to have someone who supports you in a relationship based on mutuality and mediation that can give you a fresh perspective on a difficult problem and bring you to a solution.

The big benefit of psychotherapy is that people will be able to appreciate their symptoms of distress and learn how to transform negative emotions into constructive and successful experiences. This method of talking therapy may be done on a single basis or in a group environment.

Sessions are usually 50 minutes long and take place once a week. Psychotherapy care is not only talking, but certain forms of communicating to get to the heart of an emotional problem may provide speech by music, drawing, writing and/or acting.

The idea that psychotherapy is a treatment that has relatively little side effects due to the absence of genetically modifying drugs used makes this treatment relatively attractive to other individuals. In addition to reducing psychological problems that can affect a person's life and limit his or her ability, some of the other advantages and positive benefits of psychotherapy include: 1. Developing better relationship skills.

Developing communication skills is the key to successful relationships with others. Whether it's a brief encounter or a long-term relationship, working on certain skills will make any experience more successful. Relationship skills are therefore an integral part of the development or instruction of life skills. Relationship skills are generally built on strong personal qualities, particularly good character, including integrity, trustworthiness, self-discipline and self-control (A-R-E-A of Control). Kindness and empathy are also a long way to go in building strong relationships.

Without a doubt, mutual trust and respect are the cornerstone of any successful interaction. This is true during limited meetings (sales clerks, contractors, doctors), but especially in longer-term relationships (friends, family, co-workers, partners, spouses) that involve continuous interaction. Interaction requires play on both hands. Therefore, every interaction should be a two-; a give--that involves both participants. (Again, this is particularly true in relationships.) To restate an often overlooked success secret, no one can sustain a positive relationship alone-if he or she has exceptional relationship skills.

2. Comprehending and accomplishing personal goals.

Many people feel as if they're adrift in the world. They work hard, but they don't seem to get anywhere worthwhile.

A key reason that they feel this way is that they haven't spent enough time thinking about what they want from life, and haven't set themselves formal goals. After all, would you set out on a major journey with no real idea of your destination? Probably not!

Goal setting is a powerful process for thinking about your ideal future, and for motivating yourself to turn your vision of this future into reality.

The process of setting goals helps you choose where you want to go in life. By knowing exactly what you want to do, you know where you need to focus your energies. You will also quickly spot the pitfalls that can, too easily, lead you astray.

3. It improves self-confidence.

Nobody is raised with limitless self-confidence. If someone seems to have immense self-confidence, it's because he or she has been working on developing it for years. Self-confidence is something you need to build up, because the difficult world of business, and life in general, will deflate it.

4. It combines negative thinking with positive thinking.

Bad thinking substitution is a way to reduce the sum of negative feelings in a person's mind. In the first article of this show, you heard about becoming more mindful of your negative thinking habits. In the next post, you learned how to let go of these negative thoughts when they came to you. Now, you're going to learn about the final step — replace negative thoughts with more realistic and positive thoughts.

One word of caution— if you're worried of suicide or hurting someone else, tell someone and get medical help right away.

This is a medical emergency — call 911 or support from your local hospital. Think substitution may not be enough to shield you and others from harm in this kind of situation.

5. Introducing More Optimistic: Thinking As you accept and release pessimistic feelings about your money, you will continue to bring fresh ideas into your head. Second, mention any important improvements or behavior that you and your family have taken as a result of work losses. You may have been imaginative with your schedule, sent out a lot of resumes, or adjusted any buying habits.

When you think negatively about your finances, say something different to yourself like, "I feel more in control because we've cut some of our costs," or, "We're finding ways to use our money more wisely and it helps." Use the positive information you've gained from this difficult situation to remain motivated.

6. Study relaxation techniques to deal successfully with daily stress.

While there may seem to be nothing you can do about tension at work and at home, there are steps you can take to ease the pressure and regain control.

If you're dealing with a high level of stress, you're putting your whole well-being at risk. Pain affects your emotional balance, as well as your physical health. This inhibits the ability to think clearly, to function effectively, and to enjoy life. It might seem like there's nothing you can do about pain. Bills will never stop coming, there will never be more hours a day, and the work and family commitments will always be overwhelming. But you've got a lot more influence than you might expect.

Good stress management lets you break the burden on your life so that you can be happy, safer and more successful. The ultimate goal is a healthy life, with time for work, friends, recreation and fun — and endurance to hang on to pressure and face obstacles head on. But the treatment of tension is not one-size-fits-all. That's why it's important to try to figure out what's right for you. The following tips on stress control will help you do that.

OTHER ADVANTAGES INCLUDES

- Meta-analyses of psychodynamic psychotherapy studies indicated that short-term treatment improved symptoms of depression, anxiety, and anorexia nervosa. When patients were reassessed nine months after treatment, the effect size of psychodynamic therapy had increased. An indication of lasting psychological changes that yielded further benefits as time passed

- Ongoing anger and stress are major contributors to high blood pressure and a number of related health issues. Psychotherapy produced the same level of systolic blood pressure reductions as anti-hypertension medication.

- Psychotherapeutic counseling in the treatment of heroin addiction has been shown to improve the attendance of subjects while undertaking detoxification treatment. When compared to those receiving detoxification alone, subjects receiving both treatments simultaneously were more likely to enter long-term treatment following the initial program.

- Meaning-centered group psychotherapy has been shown to reduce psychological distress and improve spiritual well-being in patients with advanced or terminal cancer.

- Psychotherapy can improve symptoms of depression, general anxiety disorder, social anxiety, bipolar disorder, OCD, phobias, and panic disorders when used as either the sole treatment or in conjunction with pharmacological treatments.

- A growing body of evidence indicates that psychotherapy decreases the use of psychiatric hospitalization and reduces the use of other medical and surgical services. Successful integration of psychotherapy into primary care may reduce medical costs by 20-30%.

- Psychotherapy in conjunction with pharmaceutical treatment has been shown to be more enduring and effective in the long-term than medication alone. The relapses of anxiety and mild to moderate depression occurred in 76.2% of those who had received medication. The relapse rate was 30.8% among those who had received medication and psychotherapy simultaneously.

CHAPTER SIX

RELATIONAL TRUAMA: PAST AND PRESENT, MEMORY AND NOW

Psychological trauma is central to the practice of all psychological therapies and is possibly one of the most frequently uttered terms in the history of psychology since its philosophical inception by the Ancient Greeks. Despite the abundance of scholarship devoted to the study and conceptualization of trauma, it remains a perplexing phenomenon given that the majority of contemporary studies focus on post-traumatic symptomatology and allied diagnostic pathology.

While the psychopathology of post-traumatic ramifications has been thoroughly examined, the pathopsychology of trauma remains an arena of ongoing exploration and debate. The purpose of the current chapter is to offer an overview of the most predominant conceptual frameworks of psychological trauma residing in the psychodynamic school of thought, which not only addresses the intrapsychic and interpersonal origins of traumatic pathology but also provides a normative framework of healthy human development.

Alongside that, a clinical case vignette will be presented to illustrate the interventions, processes, and outcome of psychodynamic treatment for complex trauma. Positioned within a post-modernist paradigm, the chapter aims to review current psychodynamic literature from a perspective that supports the notion that reality can be interpreted in multiple ways and thus embraces the diversity of multiple analytical contributions to the study of trauma.

INTRODUCTION

Derived from the Ancient Greek word 'trauma' (=wound) and preserved in its etymological originality, psychological trauma is a phenomenon that involves an injury to the psychological matter. Trauma is generally defined as any experience that is felt to be unbearable that shatters the human psychic potential and affects the human capacity to relate, and feel kinship with others authentically. According to Kalsched, trauma refers to a type of psychological injury to the capacity to feel, which occurs when we are given more to experience than we can consciously bear, especially if we the lack resources to metabolise the mental states that emerge. Such an experience may disturb our sense of inhabiting the world in a coherent, safe, and meaningful manner. As Greening quotes: when we experience trauma, our relationship with existence itself is shattered.

Traumatic experiences are broadly associated with a painful life event, which is characterised by its intensity, by the difficulty of the person to respond adequately to its sequalae and by its pathological long-lasting effects on the psychic organisation. Thus, psychological trauma is the unique individual experience of a single event or enduring conditions, in which:

(a) the individual's ability to integrate their affective experience is overwhelmed, and (b) the individual subjectively experiences a threat to life, psychosomatic integrity, or mental sanity.

The individual may be left feeling emotionally, cognitively, and physically overwhelmed, while common comorbid diagnoses associated with traumatic experiences include post-traumatic stress disorder, mood disorders, anxiety disorders, substance misuse, eating disorders and personality disorders.

The sequela of trauma commonly involves a sense of current threat, betrayal of trust, violation of psychological and somatic boundaries, loss of power, entrapment, helplessness, confusion, pain, dissociation and loss.

Broad examples of events that are associated with a traumatic sequela involve relatively impersonal events like natural disasters and accidents, or events of a personal character like many forms of abuse including psychological, sexual and physical assaults, wars and torture. Additionally, events of commission like interpersonal violation or events of omission like neglect and abandonment, which are not necessarily socially constructed as traumatic, may still result in the individual experiencing a sense of threat to their integrity.

The very fact that traumatisation is predominantly an esoteric, idiosyncratic experience renders notions of objectivity somewhat difficult to infer. For this reason, central to the formulation of traumatisation is an appreciation of the uniqueness of the individual's subjective lifeworld and the conditions that may have been shattered as a result of exposure to psychologically wounding experiences. It is the subjective experience of the objective events that constitutes the trauma…The more you believe you are endangered, the more traumatized you will be…Psychologically, the bottom line of trauma is overwhelming emotion and a feeling of utter helplessness. There may or may not be bodily injury, but psychological trauma is coupled with physiological upheaval that plays a leading role in the long-range effects.

At a neurobiological level, many studies have shown that the effects of environmental stress on the brain are being mediated through molecular and cellular mechanisms. Neuroimaging research findings found permanent structural changes in the prefrontal/frontal lobe volumes of the brain, as well as alterations in neurotransmitter systems in chronically maltreated children.

Additionally, rapid increase of dopamine under discrete or prolonged traumatic stress has been shown to cause DNA mutations in brain tissue. The main implication from these findings is that early repeated trauma may lead to permanent brain changes associated with psychopathology such as mood disorders.

Over the years, a plethora of theoretical approaches and research studies examined the immediate and long-term psychosocial consequences of intensely traumatic events, and several psychological models have attempted to conceptualise and treat clinical presentations arising from traumatic experiences. Although psychotherapies began with traditional analytic approaches, other schools of therapy have examined post-traumatic syndromes like PTSD, including cognitive behavioural therapy (CBT), existential and humanistic therapy, dialectical behaviour therapy (DBT), and eye movement desensitisation and reprocessing (EMDR) therapy. Effective treatments for PTSD include trauma-focused cognitive-behavioural therapies, psychodynamic psychotherapy, existential-humanistic therapy, EMDR as well as integrative psychotherapies.

HISTORICAL OVERVIEW OF APPROACHES TO TRAUMA

The relationship between trauma and mental illness was initially investigated by French neurologist Jean Martin Charcot, who was treating traumatized women with what was known as hysteria at the time in the Salpetriere hospital. Hysteria refers to as a set of symptoms, including amnesia, paralysis, convulsions and sensory deprivation that would usually be treated with hysterectomy. Charcot recognized that these effects may have had a neurological basis and observed that traumatic events may lead to a hypnotic state in his patients, and was the first clinician to identify the phenomenon of post-traumatic dissociation due to the persistence of insufferable encounters. Charcot's thesis, Pierre Janet, continued to study the relationship between traumatic memories and dissociation. More specifically, Janet researched the effect of traumatic experiences on the actions and growth of the personality of his patients. Janet observed a correlation between the acute effects of her patients and their recollections or perceptions of their traumatic experiences, and noticed that the symptoms of her patients had been reduced by hypnosis, abbreviation and re-exposure to traumatic memories.

A significant contribution to early trauma research was provided by the work of Freud and Breuer, referenced in the famous case of Anna O, who initially presented signs of paranoia but was later developed as a case of broken, repressed trauma arising from her relationship with her father. In their work on hysteria in 1893, Freud and Breuer alluded to emotional dissociation as hypnoid psychosis, emphasizing its relationship to a traumatic antecedent.

The introduction of hypnotic methods as an early form of treatment has led to the gradual development of a psychoanalytical approach with an emphasis on the free association, abbreviation and understanding of latent intrapsychic and emotional mechanisms as fundamental to the diagnosis of stressful manifestations such as hysteria. Acting with soldiers during World War I, Freud found that his patients frequently re-enacted their combat memories and noticed that painful hallucinations have the hallmark of constantly leading the patient back to the situation of his injury. In 1941, Kardiner, another psychanalyst dealing with U.S. victims of the First World War, also researched the effects of the trauma, and his findings were close to Freud's and Ferenczi's postulations on the existence of re-enactment, a concept relating to an implicit propensity to re-experience traumatic scripts: the participant behaves as if the initial painful condition already occurred and participatesin re-enactment.

The enormous impact of the Vietnam War on the psychological well-soldiers inspired more organized trauma studies, while increasing interest in civilian trauma, particularly abuse and domestic violence, eventually led to the development of a diagnostic classification of trauma-syndromes known as post-in diagnostics and statistics.

PTSD VS. COMPLEX TRAUMA

Post-traumatic stress disorder was initially identified as an anxiety disorder in DSM-III and DSM-IV and is characterized by an aversive perception of fear, maladaptive behavior, somatic symptoms and physiological responses that occur and evolve after an individual's exposure to a clinically traumatic event. Recent reviews of psychiatric literature also identify PTSD as trauma-related and stressor-related disorders in DSM-5. PTSD symptomatology, as illustrated in medical literature, is theorized to result in clinically significant depression or disability in several facets of daily behavior, such as employment, social relations and other key areas of day-to-day operation.

Although the diagnosis of PTSD encompasses a set of symptoms linked to post-traumatic syndromes, it does not discuss behavioral factors and childhood antecedents, nor does it provide a more nuanced and detailed understanding of intrapsychic and psychosocial stressors that have an effect on personality development and trauma-related depression or anxiety.

For this cause, trauma has been conceptualized as ontologically distinct from PTSD. According to McNally, naive realists see PTSD as an empirical, eternal, systemic psychobiological phenomenon arising in reaction to intense stressors, while social constructionists contend that it is a cultural symbol that arose in the wake of the Vietnam War. When Young cites, the condition is not eternal, nor does it possess an underlying continuity. Rather, they are bound together by the behaviors, techniques and ideologies with which they are handled, researched, managed and interpreted, and by the various interests, structures and moral arguments that organized these actions and resources.

Although trauma is always an antecedent to PTSD, both are not synonymous and it is important to emphasize that PTSD does not encompass post-traumatic symptoms in their entirety. While all PTSD patients will have undergone a form of damage at some point in their lives, not all traumatized people will continue to develop PTSD. Yehuda and McFarlane have shown that psychological trauma does not necessarily lead to PTSD but may precipitate other signs and symptoms.

The writers argue that conditions not yet fully understood assess the heterogeneity of human trauma responses. Numerous psychiatric diagnostics, other than PTSD, have been reported in traumatized individuals, including depressive syndromes, anxiety disorders, dissociative disorders, borderline personality, and substance abuse. Chertoff believes that PTSD rarely occurs on its own and suggests that a number of trauma-related psychological problems, not fully captured in the PTSD DSM-IV system, exist simultaneously, requiring a more comprehensive approach.

To addition to epistemological shortcomings and complexities in PTSD syndromes,' extreme PTSD' should be included as a new diagnosis to tackle the various causes of trauma and its effects on all areas of a person's life, including personality disorders.

According to Herman, the lack of an appropriate diagnostic definition has significant consequences for recovery, since the link between the signs reported by the victim and the stressful experience is sometimes overlooked. Attempts to incorporate patients into current medical systems generally result, at best, in an incomplete understanding of the problem and a fractured path to diagnosis.

More recently, Ford and Courtois have built a more detailed' extreme trauma ' paradigm, conceptualizing it as an inability to self-regulate, self-organize, or build relationships to restore self-integrity. Complex depression is associated with histories of multiple traumatic stressors and sensory conditions, along with severe disruptions in primary caregiving relationships.

Comprehensive definition of complex trauma also allows for a therapeutic approach that discusses acute post-traumatic effects that are not always confined or even related to PTSD but may also express themselves in other clinical presentations. In comparison, the complexity of emotional consequences is profoundly recognized within the field of human relations and characterological development. Because of the far-reaching effects of complex trauma for a patient, psychodynamic psychotherapy has been described in the literature as more appropriate for specific forms of PTSD and wider emotional trauma series.

Clinical and empiric evidence suggests that psychodynamic interventions that result in improved self-esteem, enhanced ability to respond to trauma reactions through improved reflective functioning, increased reliance on mature defenses, concomitantly reduced dependence on adolescent defenses, internalization of more stable working patterns in relationships, and improved social functioning.

PSYCHODYNAMIC APPROACHES TO TRAUMA Much of the psychoanalytical trauma literature has been based on traditional psychoanalytic theories, and subsequent developments incorporate modern psychodynamic methods arising from object-relationship and organizational psychoanalysis. Throughout psychodynamic philosophy, trauma is known to have a shuttering impact on the corporeality of the victim that needs psychological adaptation and results in distinct but polymeric psychological sequelae. Furthermore, similar to competing theories, the psychodynamic paradigm is unique in its focus on social context, unconscious behavior, and interpersonal processes.

Healthy human development during adolescence is based on a secure and stable emotional and social environment that forms the individual's intrapsychic aspects and cognitive skills. Interplay between the intrapsychicand the emotional defines, to a large extent, the nature and well-being of adults, particularly with regard to one's sense of self and the experience of the world around them.

Traumatic experiences have a unique characteristic of interfering with children's normal cognitive potential— that is, their ability to feel secure inside their psychosomatic selves and to create a sense of belonging to their human environment; to perceive and authentically communicate mental states unequivocally; to identify and react empathically to other states of mind;

Freud's psychiatric findings prompted him to theorize that intellectual life is naturally driven by two conflicting impulses — Eros and Thanatos. Eros literally translates into romantic love, Thanatos into death. For Freud, the interplay between the instinct of affection (also referred to as the instinct of life) and the instinct of death (aggression) is what triggers intrapsychic tension and causes anxiety and subsequent pathology — because it is understood through all bad feelings and disputes. Freud has selected his vocabulary with creativity. His referring to the essence of life as' Eros' was not spontaneous, as romantic love was widely regarded as the strongest of all feelings, the belief that love is one of the most basic forces in the world, if not the most fundamental, has a long and powerful history.

Ancient Greek philosopher Empedocles believed that it was by love and warfare that the four elements of nature — fire, water, air, and earth — were linked together to build all around us. Plato argued in the Symposium and the Phaedrus that love is our answer to forms— the higher level of truth, the pattern for all that exists. Plato described love as the happiness of the good, the pleasure of the wise, and the wonder of the Gods. But for Freud, the idea of love went far beyond emotional experience— it necessitated a guiding force that maintained all the positive for both identity and humanity. For Plato, it is love that leads us to the forms, the basis of reality. To Freud, whatever we try to understand and respond to, we spend in libido— in other terms, we lust. In light of Freud's focus on the essence and role of libido per se (sexual drive and its symbolic expressions), he grasped the importance of love in both intrapsychic and interpersonal terms, predicating that love and truth are at the deepest level.FREUD'S THEORY ON TRAUMA

Freud's initial seduction hypothesis postulated real sexual encounters during adolescence and early infancy as the source of all abuse and the basis for neurosis. However, he lost faith in his' seduction hypothesis' for a variety of reasons: first, he questioned the prevalence of sexual abuse he had experienced in his clinical practice, and second, during his own self-, his repressed sexual feelings towards his mother led him to recognize child sexuality as the driving force behind the development of his personality.

This revision prompted Freud to emphasize the role of latent imagination and intrapsychic confrontation over psychological influences in the production of traumatic neurosis. Freud went on to differentiate between stress and depressive neuroses on the grounds of actual experience and implicit imagination and the subsequent intrapsychic tension (e.g., desire and rage). According to Freud's psychiatric assessments, the pathogenic entity has invested in the recollection of the abuse and the victims ' protection to overcome emerging anxieties such as rejection, suppression and dissociation.

The discharged consequence of the associated painful memory typically culminated in the transition of these experiences into tolerable ordinary experiences, open to the conscious mind. However, when a reaction discharge became unlikely, these affectively undischarged memories were theorized to enter a second consciousness where they became secrets, often separated from or visible to the conscious mind in a strongly condensed manner and often unconsciously carried out.

A similar psychological finding was that of' traumatic re-enactment'—a human tendency to replicate earlier habits of interaction in an effort to overcome tension resulting from repressed, traumatic experiences. Freud described this trend in his early writings on' remembering, copying and going back' and called it a desire to repeat.

Attending the psychological practices of his patients through free association, Freud explored the concept of transference, a social phenomenon in which the psychiatrist (and other important people) symbolically portrayed a person from the patient's memory. By listening carefully to the aspects of the transference (e.g. how the patient views the client, their desires, preferences and intended roles) and slowly translating the purpose (e.g. the need to control the abusive parent by overpowering the therapist), Freud was the first clinician to relate psychological improvement to the interpersonal interaction process.

We must be prepared, however, to see that the patient yields to the urge to replicate, which now replaces the desire to recall, not only in his personal attitude towards his psychiatrist, but also in any other action and interaction that may dominate his life at that time-if, for example, he falls in love or undertakes a mission or undertakes an undertaking during therapy In addition to Freud's research, Freud's heirs, such as Klein, Winnicott, Fairnbairn and Bion, have further expanded their original model and included the field of human interpersonal relations, which is the centrality of relationships, in particular attachment mechanisms and childhood experiences, in the development of personality and character disorder following trauma.

FAIRBAIRN 'S HYPOTHESIS

A major deviation from Freud's conceptualization of libido was proposed by Ronald Fairbairn, who argued that libido was not simply pleasure-seeking but object-seeking, and that, as such, Eros could be perceived as a driving force for emotional gratification. When libidinal impulses are blocked in infancy, either by the agitation of child attachment attempts, or because the child's efforts to develop assertive and healthy relationships are not met in a mutual way by the caregivers, the child turns away from external reality. Instead of those interactions, the child develops a imaginary universe with internal artifacts that incorporates features with real-life artifacts in which the child can not develop and sustain substantive relationships.

Drawing on his research with neglected children and schizoid manifestations in adulthood, Fairbairn noted that adverse childhood experiences have led the growing child to feel unloved as a person in their own right and to perceive their own desire for parents as inherently evil, meaningless or harmful. The infant then retains the maternal characteristics and interacts with the unresponsive characteristics of the parents: lonely, anxious, masochistic, intrusive and self-destructive.

Fairbairn concluded that, by internalizing these dysfunctional traits, theinfant re-establishes a relationship with the adult that is not present in certain, safer ways. This kind of internalization of parents often inevitably produces a break in the ego: part of the self remains guided towards the real parents in the outer world, finding the actual answers from them; part of the self is diverted to the illusory parents as the inner subjects to which it is attached. Therefore, stressful re-enactmentsof future marriages were correlated with the debilitating sequelae of the object-seeking behaviour.

FERENCZI 'S CONTRIBUTIONS

Ferenczi's approach to trauma theory is similarly beneficial to exogenous interactions and their impact on the formation of personality. Ferenczi researched the patterns of relapse, recurrence and recurrence in the care of battered victims and, in addition to concentrating on the complexities of the actual traumatic interaction between the victim and the offender, emphasized another critical traumatic phase: the rejection of the traumatic event by significant persons in the child's life, particularly the mother of the child.

In Ferenczi's opinion, the external denial of the child's living nightmare was the most pathogenic factor to the degree that the child's existence became unintentionally invalidated, thereby reinforcing the dissociation and depersonalization that caused the child to resort to distorting its own reality in order to live. The problem with this type of defense is, of course, what Freud often referred to as the return of the repressed in the form of neurotic symptoms.

WINNICOTT'S CONTRIBUTIONS

To Winnicott, the perception of trauma is fundamental to the creation of a' false self,' which includes an obscured, unstable and often secret sense of identity, analogous to an insecure attachment mechanism, with an inadequate potential for confidence and honesty. Using Winnicott's words, I find it useful to divide the world of humans into two sections. There are those who have never been let down as babies and who are, to that degree, eligible for the enjoyment of life and living.

There are also those who have endured traumatic experiences of the kind that have occurred as a result of environmental degradation, and who must bear with them all their life the memories of the situation they were in at times of tragedy. These are candidates for life of storm and danger, and perhaps disease Winnicott wrote that babies begin life with an' inherited capacity' for a' true self' that represents their spiritual identity.

In the' holding atmosphere' created by the accessible, sensitive and emotionally attuned maternal figure, the child's genuine, spontaneous expressions derived from the ID are formed and their sense of identity is firmly established. Kids, on the other hand, who are subject to chronic neglect or impingement live at the cost of' eating falsely.'

For Winnicott, a false self is a required illusion for the child to put up in order to protect the mother's love by coping with her insufficient modifications or implicit desires. For example, a depressive mother may unnecessarily compel an infant to be' cheerful' and' strong' by imposing all her latent impulses for redemption upon them; a child of very violent, dysfunctional parents may be frightened to communicate any of their own negative feelings, or a child of interfering parents may be discouraged from having a capacity to be alone and to control their emotions.

Winnicott's findings profoundly demonstrate the role of emotional violence in the formation of identity, which is often insidious and unseen to' the naked eye,' as it does not inherently include the drama of sexual or physical assault and its obvious scars, but instead flows like a colorless toxin within the mental stream.

KOHUT'S SELF-PSYCHOLOGY

Kohut's self-psychology paradigm incorporates a new approach for considering normal human development and behavioral anomalies, as well as the psychology philosophy. At the heart of Kohut's hypothesis is the belief that healthy personality formation presupposes the fulfillment of key psychological needs within the attachment system, such as the need for mirroring (building a consistent sense of identity), idealization (establishing self-esteem) and twinning (fostering a sense of belonging).

Kohut viewed psychiatric dysfunction as both arising and resulting in dysfunctional self-functioning, manifesting in a variety of forms (e.g. psychotic symptoms, pathological narcissism and other personality disorders, as well as insomnia, anxiety disorders, and sexual perversions). Kohut developed these requirements as a result of recurrent, debilitating breaches of parental relations, especially empathic failures. Unlike many object-relationship philosophies in which maturation is integrated through separation and individuation, self-psychology sees the developmental continuum between self-object relationships as stretching from birth to death.

Self-psychology is therefore essentially an organizational approach that examines intrapsychic growth on the basis of how the central psychological desires of the attachment system are fulfilled.

BOWLBY'S ATTACHMENT THEORY

The roots of the attachment theory can be found in Bowlby's belief that the close proximity relationship between the child and the primary caregiver not only acts as a survival mechanism, but also helps the infant to thrive socially and emotionally. In other words, close proximity to loving parents keeps the child protected during frightening moments, while mentally providing a feeling of a' stable foundation' that encourages the child to explore the world.

Influenced by object relations, Bowlby also created the idea of internal working models (IWM) to characterize self-representational models and others focused on the consistency of early bonding experiences. Traumatic attachments marked by experiences of alienation, physical or sexual violence, neglect or parental disregard are theorized to obstruct different aspects of psychosocial development, such as interpersonal and peer interactions, impair control and damage to self-concept.

Contemporary psychoanalysts, Fonagy and Aim, coined the word ' mentalization' to characterize one's ability to perceive internal conditions in oneself and others (e.g., emotions, perceptions, expectations, and wishes) and created a hypothesis that connected inadequate emotional capability to dysfunctional self-originating, stressful attachment, interactions.

EPILOGUE: TO LOVE IS TO GIVE WHAT ONE DOES NOT HAVE

Studies with traumatized children have shown unmistakably that infants and toddlers have the emotional and cognitive ability to have lasting effects on their psyche. Traumatized children have been able to retain a form of mental reflection of their trauma for years, as evidenced by trauma-centricbehavioral re-enactment, emotional responses to traumatic stimuli, imaginative activity, tactile and somatic symptoms, and even verbal re-enactment.

Historically, a theory that has had a great deal of traction within the psychodynamic school of thought is that, in infancy, psychological trauma affects and damages growth permanently. The dominant ego of psychological trauma is theorized to exert persistent memory imprints that trigger repetitive memories, emotional re-experiencing, traumatically inducedmental re-enactments, trauma-centric thoughts, and unsettling hallucinations.

The experience is seen as having an ongoing interpersonal impact on the company over the lifetime of Gaensbauer and Jordan as a' full-edged' repeat. Analyzing the cases of traumatized adults and children, Herman concluded that, long after the trauma has passed, traumatized people are reliving the event as if it were continually recurring in the present... the traumatic moment is encoded... and spontaneously breaks into consciousness, both as flashbacks during waking states and as traumatic nightmares during sleep.

The horrific sadness of Olivia rests in the early sexual harassment she was subjected to, and although she had no memory of being sexually abused herself, the enormity of the horror she experienced destroyed her developmental capacity and the ability to form healthy relationships powered by a constant struggle between attraction and love for an object of opposition; Lacan's popular love aphorism was loving to offer what one doesn't have. To Lacan, this is the nature of love— the secret to love, to be able to love, is to recognize one's lack: one cannot love except by becoming a non-haver, even if one does.

Psychotherapy (therapeutic counseling or talking therapy) is the use of psychological techniques, particularly on the basis of daily personal interactions with others, to help a person change behaviour and overcome problems in the desired way. Psychotherapy aims to improve the well-being and mental health of the patient, to overcome or reduce troubling attitudes, values, compulsions, feelings or emotions, and to strengthen relationships and social skills.

There are also a variety of psychotherapy therapies for children and adolescents that typically involve practice, such as sandplay. Some psychotherapy is considered evidence-based for the diagnosis of some of the mental disorders diagnosed. Others have been blamed for pseudoscience.

There are over a thousand different techniques of psychotherapy, some of which are minor variations, while others are based on very different conceptions of psychology, philosophy (how to act professionally) or procedures. Most of these include one-to - one meetings between the client and psychiatrist, but some are done for classes, including relatives.

Psychotherapists may include mental health professionals such as physicians, psychologists, mental health nurses, psychiatric social workers, marriage and family therapists, or professional counseling. Psychotherapists may also come from a variety of other cultures and, depending on the state, they may be strictly regulated, willingly supervised or unrestricted (and the term itself may or may not be protected) Psychotherapy has the benefit of giving people someone to chat to. It can provide a new way to look at tough issues and help people move towards a solution.

Participants will gain a better understanding of themselves and their own goals and beliefs and build skills to improve relationships.

It can help to overcome specific problems such as eating disorders or phobias.

For psychotherapy to succeed, the client must be actively engaged and practice during the session, as well as between sessions, by learning new skills, for example.

Psychotherapy is a two-way process and there has to be a good relationship between the client and the therapist.

In order to benefit from the process, a person must first want to participate. They should then follow appointments as planned, be truthful in explaining the symptoms, and be willing to complete all set tasks.

Any clients can experience changes that they did not expect, or did not want.

Few people don't like having to relive traumatic things, but this doesn't happen in all psychotherapy strategies.

No psychiatrist can ever guess when a painful recollection will resurface, but if it does, the therapist has the ability to address the memory being remembered.

Psychotherapy may seem costly and time-consuming. When therapy is deemed appropriate, the Mental Health Parity Act mandates insurance providers to pay for mental health services in the same manner that they do for medical coverage.

However, the definition of' fair and sufficient' or' medically required' can vary.